Preface

Hello,

    This book will give you joy, love & satisfaction; but only in one condition & that is you want to accept these habits by whole heartedly. We heard about these habits from many peoples. But in this book in very simple & easy language it is explain that how can we apply these habits in our life? Also here are mentioned various methods so through that you can apply that habits in your life easily. There is so many reasons behind to write this book. One reason is this that when I decided to write a book that time these habits started to giving me the benefits. Then I decided to write on these things which is giving me the benefits & this book now reached out to you. In this book writing these habits were also useful to me; in this book writing I experienced the joy while using these habits.

    I recommend to read this book to everyone; who have at least a little wish to change his/her life.

    In this book there is so many examples are mentioned; many of them is almost true. The habits are very small, the examples are might be simple but there is so much blasting benefits of these habits.

    So let's go to change our life through good habits. These habits will not only help you to reach on top position but also strengthen you to keep that position.

    May God fulfill all your dreams & wishes.

This book is dedicate to

First of all to Bhagvan Yogeshwar (Lord Krishna). I strongly believe that I able to write this book only by his grace.

Also dedicated to:-

My parents those who are simple & targeted,

My younger sister (Dhanashri),

My 5 co-doctors,

To all my brothers in "Swadhyay Pariwar",

To all my teachers :- Daitkar Madam, Daitkar Sir, all educational teachers, Mogal Sir, Sameer Sir, Chandrashekhar Sir, Mahesh Sir, Sachin Sir & P. Shriram Sir.

To my friend Pratap & other friends also.

 May be I didn't said thanks to all in front of all; but through this book I am thankful to all you with my whole heart. Thank You.

Index

1) **Don't condemning any one. Always appreciate.**

If you really want to be successful in your life so should live without condemned any one. If you want maintain good relation with peoples or you wish to establish new relations so you need to stop condemned to people. It will be very costly, because no one likes to be condemned. Peoples are not happy to listen that someone is speaking bad about themselves. You will also dislike this that someone is gossiping about you.

What you are getting to condemning or speaking bad about someone? Definitely nothing any good. Your ego may be satisfying . May be you are thinking that you are feeling happy to do this. But that is not true happiness. False happiness is only benefit is comes from condemnation. But condemning or speaking bod about someone is very harmful. Let me clarify by few examples.

I am giving an example of a family. One passionate person borrow some money from one of his relative for his children's education; within 6 months he decided to return that money. But unfortunately by the famine & certain diseases he didn't got money of his crops. So that passionate person start feeling bad in his heart. But he returned some of that amount & said to his relative to in few months he will return rest of the amount.

Now, there is a delay comes to returning the money. But that relative starts to telling all other relatives that," I gave him to the money & still he didn't give it me back." & he also speaking something bad & condemning about that person. But to whom he was condemning about him those people was asking that passionate person that ,"you took the money from so & so person why did you not returning him?" he was saying that," I didn't think that I get my money back." After listening from all other peoples finally that passionate person decided that, "in anyhow I will never return the money to that person easily." & same was happaned. That person didn't receive his money on time. If those people come to that passionate person after listening about this he always delaying them. Now you can understand if we speak bad about someone or condemn someone it is spoiling our relation; instead of this if we appreciate to someone so our relation is always began to healthy.

There was my one friend to whom I mate in "Swadhyay Pariwar". His native & my native was very near. We had so many common friends "Swadhyay Pariwar". Whenever we mate each other sometimes we was discussing about our "Swadhyay Pariwar." But they was always appreciating to our common friends. Whenever I was mate any of them, then I was telling them that, "that brother was very appreciating to you." Very simply they was felling respect about that brother.

So many things are here to learn. Tell me if someone is appreciating yourself behind you & someone is informed you that," XYZ person was appreciating you." What will you think? Friends we want to be successful . We want keep an example in front of the peoples. We can't get anything through condemning about someone. But by appreciating we can get more joy, love & relation in our life.

Friends this incident explained me so many things. If you want to become successful so you must avoid condemning someone instead of this always appreciate to peoples. You want make respect in some ones heart about you? So you apply this habit in your life.

2) Don't underestimate yourself, keep faith on yourself.

What we are thinking about ourselves is very very important. You are only focusing on that what is less in you instead of what is more in you & how you can try to develop it & this is most important.

Many peoples are thinking like this that to do so n so work we have not enough resource & they leave it without trying. Many peoples are thinking that they want to do business but very quickly they are thinking that to start a business we need money, if we have money than we can do the business & after that they leave this business thought. Without money is unable to start a business is true only for those who don't have good habits. Those who have good habits they don't need the money to start a business. I also started my first business without money, I used someone else money.

Did you think even peacefully? Which good things are in me? What I can do more? First decide it then tell the best things to mentor or any responsible person & start to try it.

I had an business idea. I decided to start this business & sell it to whom in three months.

Then I called to my mentor & explained him that, "Sir I wish to start this kind of business." My mentor listened it completely & said, "start it my blessings are with you."   My hopes was increased & I also started my business.

After if many examples are there in front of the people they are felling less themselves. This time they are not only insulting themselves but insulting God also.

Whatever you are now you are best. But, you want know yourself. Because God made you & Gods creation is not worst. If it will be worst so we didn't call him God. We are still alive & still there will so many great things can happened through us this is very important & joyful thing for us. This kind of thought we need to keep with us.

Why does our situation is hopeless? Because we never heard the thoughts of famous & intelligent people event we didn't try to meet them. Our fellowship is with only those peoples who are same hopeless like us. Those people who never hearing the thoughts of intelligent people. We are listening from them & felling less about ourselves & become unsuccessful.

We need to listen from the intelligent peoples. Then we can come out from this hopelessness.

Lord Shree Krishna teaching in Shri mad Bhagwat Geeta, "सर्वस्य चाहं हृदयसान्निविष्टो". I am living in every ones heart. God itself is telling," Oh, you peoples who are believing on hopeless peoples believe on me & find that how much power stored in you." If God is with me so how can I be? If I am the son of God so how can I be? You will be straighten through know this truth not from listening from hopeless people.

A man can do any impossible work easily & other one can do that same impossible work easily by learning & trying. First climbing on Mount Everest was a difficult work. Now in few years so many peoples are successfully reached on it. Any work is might be look difficult but whoever is not underestimating himself can make this impossible work possible. There is so many examples in history.

Few years ago making 200 runs in ODI to only one cricketer was impossible. But when Sachin Tendulkar scored 200 runs then other batsman was also get confidence & now only one batsman can also score 250 runs alone.

This is I am telling to those who are saying that after a certain age you can't do any new thing or can't get any big achievement. 70 years old

Prabhupad was went to America with only 40/- INR to spread the principle of Bhagvadgeeta & made the difference. To teaching the principle of Geeta's to them in 10 years he built 120 temples in different countries. Various countries peoples become there disciples.

This was happened with these great peoples because they kept their faith on themselves. So you can also do so many things. You can be successful also, you just need to keep faith on yourself.

Let's take an example of Chh. Shivaji Maharaj. When they born that time who was thinking about independence (Swarajya)? May be someone was thought about it but they try for it? But Chh. Shivaji Maharaj listened the story of intelligent, brave warriors. They absorbed there qualities. They kept faith on themselves. They established Maratha Empire (Swarajya). This was our Chh. Shivaji Maharaj who made impossible to possible. Now you need to decide that to whom you need listen rather these brave, intelligent & great peoples or the other hopeless peoples & underestimate yourself. Friends the decision is in your hand.

3) Wake-up early in the morning regularly.

If you manage well so it can be very useful habit for you to wake-up early in the morning. This habit can bring a huge change in your life. So many peoples are thinking to wake-up early in the morning but this is just becoming a dream for some other peoples. Wake-up early in the morning is difficult to so many peoples. But this is also difficult to some people to wake-up more late. This is all happening because of our wrong belief.

I saw those peoples who aren't sleep more. This is not mean that they have any health issues, but that is there habit. Secondly there is a group of a peoples who are deciding so many times to wake-up early but they failed in it.

There is so many benefits of wake-up early in the morning. I also spent my time with those peoples who was waking early in the morning & feels entire day with joyful, cheerfully & pleasant. This is my wish for all of you to get this benefits. That's why I am giving some examples & some suggestions, so that you can use it & wake-up early into morning & also be happy, hopeful & get success. You have very excited for waking up early in the morning. There is two reasons are behind of not waking up early in the morning. 1)not excited & 2) you don't have any goal. If you have any strong reason to wake up in the morning so nobody can stop you to wake-up in the morning but if you don't have any strong reason so it is happening exactly opposite of this that no one can wake-up you early in the morning.

I was lost my excitement about study when I was in 10th standard. I was getting angry on those who was doing copy. That's why I was not studying well. Before the final exam my father was waking up me time to time in the night just for to study well that time. But I was again sleeping after few minutes. Only one reason behind it & that was lack of excitement in me. But after that I realized that if I was studied well so never want to avail the management quota admission facility, my lots of money could be saved.

Whenever the excitement comes in you then a very huge changes comes in your life. When I was in first semester of diploma that time there was 5 Doctors was my roommate. Dr. Mahesh in one of them told me," see Akash you are living with us. If didn't score well so it will be shameful for us. Your father will say that, "even Akash is living with you he fail or he didn't score well." So to avoid this situation you must have to study well. If you don't understand so ask to us. Any one from us will guide you. Go into tuition, but do your study."

Then I started to go into the tuition. As like them I started to woke up in morning 8 a.m. & came back late on the room. Suddenly excitement starts to flow in me. My goal was fixed. I want passed by good marks. I was passed in first year by the guidance of all Doctors. I can manage my time very well . I was inspiring for my study to watching them to doing there studies.

Few days I was lived in "ISKON TEMPLE" with some religious & unmarried people. I found that unmarried peoples are more educated. So many of them was engineer. They all was starts waking up from morning 3 a.m. Me other few boys was waking up on 4 a.m. The goal was fixed of all. In the morning attending "Mangala Aarti" at 4:30 a.m. even you slept in the night late or not. Going to attend the "Aarti" & meeting to God that was very joyful for them.

Whenever we need to go to outstation or for a picnic that time we need to the alarm? Definitely Not.

Following tips will useful to you but for that you need to be consist which very important:-

1)   Fixed a time when you want to wake up. To The God to whom you worship pray to him that, "God please help me to wake-up in the morning on (your decided time)." Before go to the bed in night. 4 to 5 times pray this & give thanks to him & sleep quickly. If you have full faith so you can wake up on same time without alarm. Same time your eyes will be open.

2)   If you want to be so much cheerful, so do that work which would you like to do means whichever work feels you joy to do so much so do it after waking up. Fixed the time in the morning to do that work. Because we are never getting bore in our favorite work. You will be so much excited to do your favorite work & to do that work you will be easily wake up.

3)   You set your goal & do it as you make a plan to complete it. Create urgency for complete that goal.

4)   Keep the same ringtone of your alarm & incoming call. So that when alarm will ring you will think that your phone is ringing & you can wake up that time.

5)   Give prize to yourself.

6)   Don't use your Mobile & Laptop at least 1.5 to 2 hours before you go to sleep in the night.

7)   Get the help from your parents. Tell them to wake up you on fixed time in anyhow.

Any tip from above you like that you can apply. Don't apply all tips. You constantly try to this for 21 days. If you miss a single day so you have to start it from again first day. Which day will delay to wake up that you have to read 5 pages of any book as a punishment.

This is very interesting. You will get joy in this. Once you starts to wake up early in the morning then you can't sleep any more.

4) <u>**Do Exercise regularly.**</u>

Did you know? Your exercise or maintaining your health is very useful to your success. If you really want to become successful so you must do exercise. To getting the success you want to do some work but to do that your body & brain must support to you. That's why to keep your body healthy you need to do exercise. To reading the books you can do exercise of your brain.

Actually we deciding to do exercise but we fail to keep it constant. But we need to keep it, because we want to be successful. You fixed a time to do exercise & that time you only do the exercise. For that you can wake up early or you can keep some time in the evening. If you want do exercise regularly or you have the habit of exercise so must fix a time for your health.

Keep this in your mind that anything can be happen I will do exercise on a fix time. You need to make a strong desire for the exercise, then it will be possible to you to do the exercise. There is so many peoples who are deciding to start the exercise from next day & next day they are not waking up, if they wake up but they are going to busy in other work.
There is one reason behind it that is they only know that through the exercise there body will be healthy but they don't realize that exercise is also important in success. Your body will be always fresh & healthy by exercise, it will help you to do more work. If you will be fresh then you will be think creatively & you can find new concepts & make a best example. By the exercise you will become active, always be cheerful, so you must need to do exercise. Let see some examples that which kind of reasons are peoples giving & how can we avoid it.

Once I was watching a South Indian movie, in that movie there was an action scene; hero was beat the all villains. After some time I went to just walk to out. There was two groups was fighting with each other. But other peoples solved it. That time I was thinking "Oh God if my body will be strong so I could beat to 10/15 guys & fighting which they was thinking like as a joke so I will clear them. But then thought from next day onwards let starts to exercise & find Karate training class. But it was not decided by whole heartedly next day I thought " I am so clever. I am not arguing with anyone & if it will happen so I am able to clarify to others that they are wrong, so this way doing exercise is stopped. Sometimes there was not enough money to join the gym & if money will come no time was left for that. But if you have a desire to do exercise so you can make it your habit. I am not telling you to expense your money. Wherever you are living in that city there is a small garden is available, there is a green gym, you can do exercise there. If you are married & you have small children's you can take them with you & everyone can do exercise. With your children's will also learn to do exercise & this is so much important for them.

See your one decision can make the difference. But for this you need to keep a desire. You have to decide that you want to become successful or not.

I have my one friend, he was told me that," first we have to become successful after that we can entertain ourselves. " I said," you are right my friend. But are you coming tomorrow with us for exercise?" he replied, " No this year only I will do only study & nothing else." I said, " but if we didn't do exercise now so when you will be grown you will be fall seek & whatever money you will be earn you will send it all to recover from that." He was agree & I was also but we didn't do exercise or study. This kind of discussion is always happening in childhood but nothing is coming out of this.

This will be so interesting but these are true examples. After always neglecting we are not taking care of our body & suddenly when we suffered from any disease we waking up. That time our time & money both are left. May be you heard that opportunity is never coming to inform us & it is coming on that time when we can't grab it. So that's why we have to keep maintain our body healthy & we always get ready for any opportunity. We can do exercise in anyhow. But exercise is become our need. We learn to love ourselves, then we can learn to take care of our body.

To apply this habit we can do the any of following non expensive tips like:-
1) Use to green gym.
2) Go to the morning walk
3) Walking make our habit
4) Keep walk away if distance is short
5) Use the stair case
6) Do exercise regularly
7) Make new friends
8) Love to yourself, may be it is not sustainable but till it is with us we need to take care of it that is duty.

5) <u>Be always thankful to God & other people from the depth of your heart.</u>

This is not so easy to giving thanks as we think. Sometime the situation is comes like you want to say thank you to someone is very important but you forget. So you must apply this habit of giving thanks. Every morning after waking up I am giving thanks to God. This is my words are, "Thank you God for this new day. I am feel glad for whatever I have." Showing gratitude is a formality, a moral value. Gratitude have more importance in our culture. There is forgiveness for all sins but not for ingratitude. You are giving thanks for all small small things so are we showing gratitude to that power means God who is taking care of us? If you are not doing that so start it from today even now you should have to show your gratitude.

Your parents are working for you so much did said them thank you separately? If not so you can say it now. At least once show your gratitude for them with whole your heart. You will feel joy 100 times more than them. It is common to fill shy in starting; but this is so much important for you.

You should be thankful for your teachers, because of them you know the words.

Each one of them is your teacher who guide in your life, you should have to be thankful for them. Why does you need to make it your habit? Let see,

1)   Do you want to be successful/
2)   Do you want to make progress in every area of your life?
3)   Do you want to make your relationship much stronger?
4)   Do you want to improve you communication skills?
5)   Do you want to make your personality memorable?
6)   Do you want that peoples have to appreciate to you?

If the answer is "YES" of all above questions so this habit is more important for you. Giving thanks is like a miracle.

How can you make this habit more better, here are some tips:-

1) Whenever you giving thanks to someone so give it from the depth your heart.

2) Use different tone for giving thanks.

3) Be thankful as per situation.

4) Show different expressions on your face.

5) Use proper body language.

6) Please mention in your daily diary to whom you gave thanks on that day.

Few years ago so many times I was thinking that the person in front of me may be feel bad after my thanks giving or that person will think that this is saying it selfishly. I face trouble of my runaways & inferiority complex. I failed to be thankful to so many peoples. Now I am thankful to every person who came in my life with whole of my heart, thank you.

6) <u>Laugh & make it others to laugh</u>

It is fine if you don't have anything but a smile is must need to come on you face, also if you know the art of making others to laugh so it is better. It is best of best part of life that you know to make others to laugh.

There is so many benefits of laughing but ask this only to whom who know about it. That person who never ever laugh in his life he will tell you, " brother this laughing n all is just a myth it is very difficult to survive. Every foot step you will get the peoples who are making trouble to you, distraction is coming, this problem will become that kind of problem will come." They can see only problem & problem everywhere & they are always crying. They are also telling to the peoples to cry, n there is no any other option without cry. If this is the problem so how can we laugh?

This peoples don't know when & how to laugh? They are always crying. If the person is once start to cry then he can't laugh. If someone laugh so they getting anger on him. We don't need to change forcefully. But if you really never want to crying, you want joy & give joy to others so you once experience this habit. See what is changing in your life. I am giving you some real life examples which will give you an idea. May be these are simple but you must read. You have to laugh & make it others to laugh this is God's will.

I was in the third year of diploma that time one madam was taking a lecture. I studied on that subject in my tution class so I know the topic very well. That day there was 12/15 boys & 5 girls in our classroom. No one was interested to listen that. We all was continuously laughing in that time, so that's why she asked us a question. She asked one by one. I was confident about that answer. In this kind of time anyone can be happy. Coincidently those girls & I was left to the answer but madam gave first chance to them. One of that girl was so excited, she want show herself important or smart. But unfortunately she gave wrong answer & I laughed so loudly. I stopped laughing in between & others starts to laughing. She felt insult, she starts to cry & she shouted on me. She said, "if you know the answer so say it why are laughing on other." I replied quickly, "I didn't laugh on you." But she was getting more angry & finally madam sort it out.

The reason behind of this example is that this is important that we have to laugh by the situation. But we need to laugh is important.

So many times we experienced in our classroom, when any teacher is laughing or we are learning with laughing that time we are quickly understand it. There was my sir to whom I am taking as my ideal, his name is Mr. Mogal sir. He was making so much entertainment while teaching. His some dialogs was attracting to subtends & atmosphere was began to change. Once a man feels joy to do something than that thing will become so easy. I learned this from sir. There is so many benefits of laughing & making to laugh, isn't it? His one dialog was so much famous & every students like it. If any topic was looks like difficult so to make it easy needs to create different ideas. It is need to do more in Math's & Physics. On that time it was a magic spell to make difficult thing into easier. Students was asked, " what is this sir?" so sir was replying, "this is of God.' This dialog was motivating to students again & subtends was understanding that this is constant or this topic is not so much important. There was my one friend from Kerala & he newly came to stay in my room. When he was new that time I was not staying more in the room due to my busy schedule. We was not gathering more & he was also staying alone there. Then whenever I was meeting him that time I was talking with him joyfully. " how are you my friend? How was your day? What you did today?" or some time I was appreciating him with a smile. He was also feels to joy. If we talk with someone smilingly so we are feeling better but that person also feeling the same. We can be friend together.

If feel hopeless, sad or busy somewhere; so there is a very simple tip for you, if you see any small children so give them a smile, they will also smile. One day I was going to meet my one friend by local train. I was watching cricket match on my mobile. There was no tension if there is a match going on. I was seated in local train & there was a family seated in front of my bench. Two ladies, one young boy & two small girls with also one little boy was there. Approximately they all kids was 3-4 years old, I just looked to her casually. I smiled towards her she also smiled & I was busy again to watching the match. When ad came I just looked to her slowly so she stood up with her little brother & I was thinking that they both are waiting for my smile. And same was happened. I smiled to them & they all three kids was started to laugh loudly. It was going around 15-20 minutes. Very funny incident it was but I want drop down there otherwise I was not sure about that till how much time I has to be laugh. They all 3 kids was laughing very loudly. If we placed a smile they was starting to laugh. Ha.ha..ha… ha.ha..ha…

It was so joyful, their parents & other people was in the train was also laugh so much. So many peoples can laugh by our one smile.

The positive energy is generating by your laughing. Confidence is building up by laughing. Laughter is a weapon. It may be use in the right place, on right time & for right work & get the right fruit. Laughter is good for that's entertainment industry is so huge. If there is a human so there is emotions, where is emotions there is happiness, sorrow, love, success, & failure etc. will be there. So why not we can increase the joy of our & other peoples? We are the leader. We are taking the work. From today onwards you have to decide that you will make someone laugh without any selfishness & only for his joy. But not to the same person. Every day only one person but different one may be there is any Man or any Woman. After few days you will feel that how much you are changed. You will call a "The Happiest Person" by the people. You will definitely be a happiest personality. Your tension will run away. People will ask you that, " how are you so happy?" people will respond you that you are so good, so happy, you are doing well, etc. & will bless you; your life become so much prosper. Laughing & making others to laugh is only done by some quality people, not any one can. I have full faith, if you are reading this book so you are the quality persons.

Laughter is free & in this world those things are free it means those things are getting from to the nature that is so precious more than any other things. Like, the air, water etc. these kind of things same is your laughter as well; as but so much precious.

7) <u>Take an initiative while talking</u>

This habit will bring so much change in our life; also bring so many other opportunities. It will help to make your life more easier & happier. Also this can help you to grow you in your personal level & if you really want to become successful so you must need to make it habitual & you will find that those things was looking impossible for you they are now possible for you.

I will explain you that by how this one habit so many think of views can change. How can we starts to think on higher level. Once we starts to think on high level than we are inspiring to do right things. We can got the right peoples once we can starts to do right things. Finally the success is getting us.

Here I am giving you my personal example,

Sometimes I couldn't speak. I can't able to explain my self; it was difficult to me to what should I have to say to the person in front of me?

When I was working in a placement agency some boys was gossiping against me to my parents; my parents had trust on me. But so many times they boy was adding some other story in my matter; that my parents was asking me, " son is this true? What is this actually? Tell us; we can only understand if you say to us."

But after listening this I don't want to talk with them because there was a good intention behind my every step, then after all of these accused I don't want to talk anymore.

My parents lost their trust on be because I was not talking Of course it was naturally. But I was thinking that my parents know that how I am? But instead of this they are showing disbelief on me. Then after all of this I was praying to God & just listening all of these nonsense.

One time has come that our relation was so much damaged. I was thinking to committing suicide, I was thinking to leave them & go so far somewhere but by the grace of God I was in the fellowship of good peoples, good community & good mentality. These kind of thinking starts to inspiring me to become successful.

I will become so much successful if I told my feelings in the very beginning. Why does I failed to spoke? Because I was thinking that I am a very simple, passionate person. My motive was not wrong ever. So whatever I am doing in that I am not wrong so my parents or any other should understand me, but this was silly to think like this; because how can peoples understands about your purpose behind your action either the results of your behavior or when you will speak. The results was not coming quickly in my life & I was not speaking, so then mind was not cleared. In result of this that the feeling of guilty has comes permanently. So dear readers try to learn to make your mind clear.

That time I didn't understand but now when I understand after thinking on this that if I spoke in very starts, if took a decision on that time so from there onwards I will be 15 years more advanced. Why 15n years? Because of my this mistake I could not make my habit of speaking , & for without this habit the person is not interested in his life. Without interest no target & without interest there is nothing to do. This is not true that I can't do now what I could do that time. Still I am doing that & this book is the result of that. But whatever is changed is the peoples & the situation. But today I have this habit. I learned this by my action. This is amazing. Today I have various true experiences that can solve any kind of problem.

Through this example I don't want to explain my painful story but I want to say that only to take an initiative & speak. Make your mind free otherwise there is only repentance left behind.

When I was started my new company there was my one friend Pratap. Pratap was taking 'Animation Classes', we was good friends. Sanjay was my another friend, he wants to become a trainer. Everybody can face the financial problem so we decided to tell Pratap to desine the poster. Because we no need to do hurry for the payment & in that we can get the good quality.

After giving the work to Pratap almost after one month Sanjay came back & collect the poster after doing some changes he want. When Sanjay mate him he directly ordered to male the poster without asking him about the cost or the payment even formally. Pratap called me & told about all of this, I asked Paratap that he even asked to Sanjay for the bill? He replied 'No'. that time he want just a formality instead of payment. Because he was thinking that Sanjay's mentality is only to completing his work.

I told to Pratap that, "you are also right but you need to ask him for the money. Because you are doing the work." My intention was only to make a fine deal for both of them. Because Pratap was also doing his work very honestly that I know personally. He is new but he is making new ideas & Sanjay also want to come in the training newly, he is also not so much rich. But after all finally Pratap took initiative to talk & he got his money.

Here I want to mention one thing that is if we take an initiative in talking we can avoid the suffering & the work we suppose to do it is become easy & quickly.

8) <u>Write your daily diary through this way</u>

If you really want to become successful early so you must write a diary. But many peoples are thinking that to writing a diary in that we want to mention all of that what was happened in that day. Many peoples are so much negative. Many peoples are thinking that to writing a diary is very childish. Because I think they don't know the benefits of how to write it? There is so many benefits of to writing a diary. We are searching slowly ourselves. We are checking ourselves & we are finding that we are on the right track or not. We get joy. We can understand our mistakes & it will become easy to work on it. Our productivity is improving. We become more enthusiastic. Our work can inspiring us to make it more better. We should apply this good method for all of us. The diary which we going write that we can use for to keep the track of the progress in our daily life. We can shortlist the activities which we are using to develop the various part of our life. In this diary you can keep the things as possible as.

Use the following methods to write the diary:-

1) Avoid to write the whole things which was happened in whole day, you will be bored from this, instead of this only mention the whole thing which was happened good with you.
2) Today which good work I had done? What good thing I did? Write it. Appreciate yourself for that & must give the thanks to God for that.
3) Try to learn any special art every day. What we are learning every day? Write it that. To learning about to developing your personality, the target you had decided in a special art,

For example:-

You want to make the habit of reading the books, so you need to decide that daily you will read the book at least 10 min. but suppose if you forgot to read the book in whole day, so you can realize it while writing the diary that you are truly working on yourself or not?

4) Today to whom I had make it laugh? Ask this question everyday & write the answer honestly.
5) Make list of you next day work & also check the list of that day works. Today which work I completed & what is left to do?
6) What am I learned from what I had done today? Try to make a conclusion.

9) <u>Make a new friend everyday</u>

To increasing your network is very important for you to become successful & you should make it your habit. Our teacher Mr. P. Shriram was saying that, "one hello make a new friend."

It easy to make a new friend. There is so many peoples are traveling in the bus, train or everywhere in the traveling. If you become the successful so they never talk to you by themselves. Because they don't know that you want to become successful, but if you want to become success & you know that very well; so you need to start to talk with them. When you starts to talk with them then they will also starts. Many peoples are fearing to talk. I was also, but our sir was always saying that, " your network is your net worth." That means you will become more successful as much as your network is big.

Once you starts to talk with unknown persons, you try to talk 4-5 peoples your fear will be run away automatically.

For example:- I was staying in the ISKON TEMPLE that time we was promoting about one workshop. We confirming the peoples entries by explaining them about the workshop. For that we went to the railway station. We was meeting any boys or girls & introducing them from where we are from & explaining them about the workshop. So many thoughts was coming in mind before starting. What peoples can talk about us? If anyone can see us? If anyone insult us? If anyone laugh on us? & many more. But I start to try it keeping all these thoughts aside. First I failed. Second time I was little bit successful. In all of this activity I faced insult also & this insult is become very useful to develop our skill. I feels after that if I keep doing this few more days so my skill will developed much more & I can call so many peoples in this workshop.

Take an initiative by yourself & make new friends. The network is very big of successful peoples. I decided to start the business without money, that time my network was become more beneficial to me. My friendship was with so many new peoples, those are very expert in their respected sectors. I built up a new business with the help of them without no money.

Mr. Mahesh ji is one of my friend, he is never missing to attending any workshop. He is going to every workshop which he know & making new friends, that's why his network is become bigger & it will beneficial to him to start a new business. He is always ready to increase his network, for that he is not waiting for anyone. He is taking an initiative in himself. You can also take it, make new friends.

Use the following tips:-

1) Take initiative. "One hello makes new friends."
2) Built up the relation with the peoples with whole heart.
3) Enroll in every program, lectures & workshops.
4) Join a business group.
5) Use social media.
6) Take initiative talk with the peoples, know about themselves & their business, tell them about yourself spontaneously.
7) Learn the communication skills.

10)   <u>Take decisions & responsibility quickly</u>

We want to become successful, for that we need to do something. But we are not taking a decision or delaying for it. If you are doing this you will realize that someone is doing that before us & being successful & after this there is nothing left instead of repent. The reason behind this may that the time which we are taking in during to making the decision & our carelessness. If you want to become successful so you need to make the decision very quickly. In any sector wherever you want to become successful so decision making is very important. Let it become wrong but take it. If your decision will become wrong so you can face failure & in that you can develop the art of decision making.

Many peoples are thinking that I need to take a good decision. But why should not their decisions are being good? Anyone can take a bad decision for itself? Decision is not good or bad. We need to convert that decision into good decision by working on that decision. But when you will do something only then your decision will be good.

For example:- if a lady had 80 kgs. weight. She want to reduce 10 kg. She told me that, " Akash ji I want to reduce at least 10kg of my weight. But from last 1 year since I decided it could not happened." I replied that, " Madam are the prime minister?" she asked, "why?" I replied that, " you will take decision & can other will work & you didn't? I didn't saw anyone who can't reduce at least 10kg in year ever." She replied very honestly on it that, " yes I was decided it, but didn't try for it." Does your condition like this, isn't it? Today this is very important that we need to take decision very quickly.

I heard this in one seminar that, a businessman was taking to the decision for doing his any work & then he was organizing all things for that. The only important thing is for us that he is a very big businessman.

We are only thinking that we will do this after it will be done. But the friendly situation couldn't be make. Someone else is making it through to taking the right decision & becoming successful. Then we are saying that, "that was not for us." To hide our failure we are blaming on the fortune.

Once you took decision so whatever you supposed to do so do it. You can say this to yourself that ," I can keep on going to reach out to my goal." Then take a decision & keep working on it constantly, see the success is waiting for you. But for that you need to take a decision. Decide to do new various things & make it fast.

Lots of well wishes you for that!

11)   <u>A faithful guide (teacher/mentor) is important in our life</u>

The guide is the important part of life in many successful peoples. It quite be difficult to be successful without any guidance. But if you have a guide then it's very easy to become successful.

Very simple example I am giving. We born that time our parents are our firs teacher. If they doesn't taught us what should be happen? They taught us to speak, to walk. They taught us the morals so that our life becomes happier. Then next in the school through our teachers we can learn about the words.

In whichever sector we are we need a teacher. The teacher is not only in the spiritual sector or he may be not a person with long beard. In every sector of life like spiritual, emotional, financial, social, corporate & all other sectors the teacher is very important. The one thing is good for us that we can found the teacher in all of these sectors. We just need to go to them. We can take a guidance in any problems of our life. I am explaining you the benefits of this habit that by the teacher we can make our life happier & get right direction for our life.

Many peoples are saying that they don't need a teacher, I know everything, whatever I will do it will be right. But I am saying you must need a teacher. Let see some examples of some great & successful peoples, those who was very great & still they are. But they had a teacher.

1)	Sachin Tendulkar
2)	Indian Cricket Team
3)	Bill Gates
4)	Warren Buffet
5)	Arjun
6)	Milkha Singh
7)	Merry Kom

Even Arjun had a teacher. Having a teacher it helps to Arjun to become a greatest archer. On kurukshetra he had accepted the guidance of Lord Shree Krishna & won the crusade. If the Lord Shree Krishna doesn't entered in Arjun's life as a teacher so even after a greatest archer Arjun never fight the battle or won it.

If these kind of great peoples need a teacher so the peoples who want to become successful in life like of us we must need to a teacher; so that's why the teacher is important in our life.

I am telling you an example of the importance of the teacher in the business. Four youngsters mate a business coach & said to him, "we want to become successful in our life, we want to become successful in the business. We strongly believe that you can help us." They youths was not so much educated, their family condition was also so much bad; but they had a huge willpower. The coach said, " my fees is too high." He gave them a fix timeline to pay the fees. That youths had a huge willpower. They arranged the amount of fees. The coach was amazed that how they did paid the fees? The coaching has started. The coach told them to giving them a target," see in this 1 month if you sell out these all plots so I could be continue the coaching otherwise I will stop it." That coach thought that one of them to be able to sell maximum 8 plots; so if everyone can be sell 8 plot each even the could not sell it all. But they had full faith on the coach, they want to become successful, they want to learn. In only 22 days they sold out 500+ plots.

This is an example which very inspirable to all youth as well as to the all businessmen. There is lots of examples. I mate so many coaches they had so many teachers. They are taking training on regular basis. They had spiritual mentors, business coach, mind coach, communication coach, fitness coach.

The teacher is must be successful. Don't make anyone to your teacher. Take guidance from only anyone who is the working in that sector or he is successful in that sector. If you take guidance from those person who doesn't know anything you will be unsuccessful. So be careful about to choosing the teacher. The teacher is always save us from the loss.

You need to God or the success in the life the teacher or the mentor is must needed. That's why in our culture we are giving the honor of God to the teacher. "गुर वदेवो भव: " "गुरु: साक्षात परब्रम्ह " the teacher like the God this is our belief. If your goal is small so the teacher will help you to complete it but he also will give you the big goal & make it complete by you, this is also true.

12) <u>Wearing good clothes to feel good to self</u>

If you are a businessman so you must need to wear good cloths which is very important. You might be a businessman, an officer or a student t you must need to wear good cloths. To wearing good cloths its never mean that you need to wear costly cloths. Good cloths means they must be comfortable to you.

You have so many cloths but none of them is ironed or washed, so tell me which dress you will wear? No one & if may be you wear it so did you feel that is no need to tell newly & how many peoples become your friend or how many peoples feel happy to see you? To wearing the cloths to make peoples happy this is not I mean to say. What my say that take 2-4 but good & affordable cloths & use it; so if you will go somewhere out so you no need to feel shy. Once I went to meet my one friend; I traveled by train for 2 hours; so much rush was there. We discussed almost 4-5 hours & after that he said, " whenever you will go to meet any businessman so your cloths must dressed well. It's may be ironed, should alert that which watch are wearing, shoes must be good & polished. If you will look good so anybody can say you to seat otherwise no one can't.

I agreed with his statement because that day had no money so that's why I wore the cloths without ironed. I wore the T- Shirt of 100/- Rs. My belt was also not good, my shoes was muddy, my hair was whiskered. I decided before & after that, that was I keep ourselves as good as possible. If I had money so I was wearing the cloths after ironed. This is not for show-off to the peoples but our satisfaction. This is very is very important for all of us. No one can come near to you to talk if you attained any seminar, wedding or any other program with the cloths without ironed, unclean; if you will go so nobody can show you the interest. You can experienced it. May be many of you experienced it, I also. But have you ever experienced that your confidence is increased if you wear the cloths which are good & your favorite isn't it? Surely you experienced. While talking with someone frankly that time the strength within you is increasing more. You are talking with them too much or the peoples encouraging to your speech/responding well. They also would like to talk with you this is also I experienced; that's why I am telling you.

Our sir was telling us that peoples are saying this, " the life is must be like simple living & higher thinking" this is true, but in today's world higher living is also important as higher thinking as. We need make an example by living good & thinking high for become successful in the life.

I was living with celibate & religious peoples for so many days. These peoples thoughts are higher, their lifestyle also. They didn't have any kind of temptation but they doesn't wearing the cloths which once they used it; so many reasons behind that. But I only want to say that we have to wear clean, good & ironed if possible cloths. Keep the lifestyle which pleases you. Develop ourselves & our business & make the difference & also help to who is doing this.

I am telling you an example just for fun, once there was a time when I had less or no money, so that time I was going to any hall which was in 1-1.5 km from my residence for to attained the program for eating food. I got complete food & money was also saved. I was talking with very confidently. I was talking with anyone of them but peoples didn't realized this that I am not of in the program. Because my cloths was good & my talking was also good, that's why my so much money was saved. I know that so many guys are doing this. Mostly I saw the students of engineering. This is wrong. This is also effecting in our life. So that's why I stopped it after realized it. human loves the cleanliness. Cleanliness is must be a quality. Moral of this is only that be clean & healthy & surely become successful.

13) <u>Keep the names of peoples in the mind & call them by their names when they meet</u>

The person to whom loving so much is itself. Are you become successful, for what? What is the reason behind it? because you want to prove yourself that you are something, you are important, you want make your name memorable, the every generation from your family need to remember you. Many of these kind reasons are behind it & these belongs to your name. you have some name & you will become known by your that name & achievement. If you did some good works for the peoples in your hometown & I wish to tell that others so how did I say this? I must need to use something so that to whom I say this he will know you.

Did you know that knowing unknowingly everyone is loving so much on his name & if we can remember their names so that we can improve our relations very well. When you are calling someone by his name then that person feels like he is important, then he can do something for us that is more possible. If you have some peoples under you for work so you call them by their names & tell them your work lovingly. See they will do it very honestly & you will get good output.

If your friend meets you after a long time & when you appreciate or welcomes him by his name so see how much he feels happy for that. He feels that ' how much good friend is this! After so many days I am meeting him & he remembered my name, the friend is to be like this.'

The peoples who are successful, more of them are using this habit. Because they know that the peoples have value for their name & we can also become successful by using this habit. We can also make our life an ideal for others. We also become successful, effective by using this habit of remembering the names of the peoples.

14)   <u>Love to yourself</u>

To love to yourself is not simple as we say. Really are you loving yourself? You will say what question you are asking? We are loving ourselves.

It is good if you are loving. But if we are loving to someone so we are ready to do the best of best & we are doing it also. Whatever is possible to do we are doing it but impossible also. So you say are you loving yourself so why are you addicted by bad habits? Do have any bad addiction?

You don't have good habits it means you are not loving yourself. From today, now, immediately ask the question to yourself that, "am I loving to myself?"

15)   Attached with any organization/community/group (At least one)

You need to attached at least one with any community/organization/group. The benefits of this is that our network is expanding & we can do some social work. We can realize the hidden skill in us. If we don't know any skill so we can learn that by observing them.

When I went to Nasik after closing my classes, that time I decided to not talk more with anyone, no more new contacts. But the result of all of this that after few years I faced difficulties during the conversation. I know how to talk with someone but I can't talk. After for this reason my financial condition drop down & I lost the opportunities which was coming towards me.

I stayed in ISKON TEMPLE for few days. That time I learned some communication skills from those celibate & devotee peoples. I have a friend who's name is Pratap, he was mate me there . I also learned the communication skill from him.

After that I starts to go into the "Swadhyay Centre" regularly. I was became fan of everyone. They peoples are talking with so much love. I was doing the same which I was already doing, but I also learned so many things & I assimilated that quality of them. I am attached now with the group of "Happy Thoughts." They peoples are also talking with so much love. Their communication skills is also awesome. Not only one of them but all had good communication skills also. We can also learn.

I served in the Ashram of happy thoughts by using these all skills, that time so many peoples gave me the compliment & I gives all credits to the God & all above mentioned peoples. Because of them I renewed. You also join any group, but joining is important. More than this I wish to say that don't just join but attained their various programs, part take in it & see you will find that knowing unknowingly trying to make yourself successful. Probably you will meet so many good peoples in these places. Suppose you are doing a business, you want to expand it but you don't have any partner or enough money, so what will you do? So you visit to a business group. They are organizing the meetings, attain that meeting, describe about your business. If anyone could be interested so you can get the partner or investor. If you are a investor so in these group you could get a person with highly profitable business idea. Personally you are learning so much & you will experienced the happy moments while working in that.

Would you like to learn more? If the answer is yes so as Chanakya said, " if you are learning from others mistakes, so that you can learn from various peoples from these places." Superb habit is it, isn't it? truly very good habit. You can try it. You will feel joy.

16)   <u>Do the meditation on a certain time regularly</u>

Did you know that how much the benefits of the meditation? You must be read & may have heard about the benefits of the meditation, many of you experienced of it. I think that if we starts to the meditation by honestly so we can enjoy the benefits of that.

There is lots of spiritual benefits of the meditation (Dhyana). Your mentor can explain well of these more than me. We can reached to the highest stage in the spiritual life. I am telling you the benefits to become us to successful other than spiritual benefits.

That is good if you are doing the meditation (Dhyana). But if not so please decide to do it from today & now onwards.

Now you are thinking that how to meditate? So the answer is very simple that you just go on Google or Youtube & find out the videos on it. if it doesn't like or understand so seat at any silent place, close your eyes & concentrate on your breathing. Do it for 10-15 mins. In starting. Slowly increase the time when you feel joy. You will have fun. You will experienced that you are become happy. Your concentration is increasing, your peace of mind is increasing, if you are angry so your anger is decreasing.

There is so many methods of the meditation, you can learn any one of them. You can meet the notable spiritual Gurus or the trainers. You can learn from them.

You will be find that your worries are less in few days when we are meditating. Otherwise today so many peoples are worrying unnecessary. Because of that mental satisfaction is effecting, worrying unnecessary is harmful for our spirit. The results of that our body is also effected, in that headache, stomachache, backache etc. & so many other disease starts. That is our loss, so that's why if we make these habit so we can fight these disease thorough that habits.

I know many peoples in my contact who are meditating regularly, I also heard their experiences. Their life is become more beautiful more than before. Their relations are also beautiful. They are also facing the problems, but now their attitude is more beautiful to see that problems. They are responding well in problems & try to convert that problem into the opportunity. They are being happy in all conditions. It's all could be happen by the meditation. Your life can be change. You just try for it. But you try honestly so that you can get some good results.

17)   <u>Always read new books, read at least 30 mins.</u>

Everyone will tell you to read the books. But nobody can tell that which book you need to read? In which sector you are working or want to work so read the books related to that sector. There is so many masters in your field so you can ask them & take their guidance.

I can strongly recommend that we need to read the books on self-empowerment with the educational syllabus. So that's why we can learn new skills.

You must be read the books at least for 30 mins. We must need to read the books for the development of our life. We can learn the various skills from various peoples by reading the books. By reading their autobiography we can develop our life by applying their habits. Many peoples are saying that they are falling asleep while reading the books. You want to become successful? So read it in standing, even still you falling asleep, so you can read while walking, you can read with taking tea, do anything but read the books. If you can read the book regularly till 8-10 days so you will feel so much joy. I experienced it. reading the books it means more knowledge in less amount. If you are read the reading the book half an hour daily, so trust me you will be 6 months ahead from your friends who are not reading the books. You will find yourself changed.

If you are reading the book every day for 30 mins., so every month it will be 900 mins. 900 mins. Are means 15 hours. How many books you can read in the 15 hours? So many.

Read the books on self-empowerment. Stories, novels are not might be become so useful.

    1)   Keep any book with you & read it when you get the time.
    2)   Make it your habit to read at least 30 mins.
    3)   If you doesn't like to read the books so listen it. now audio books are also available, till here you will get the summery of the books.

18)   Don't compare

This is the special habit of everyone. You will become sad if you keep comparing & never become successful. If you will be the richest person of the world, more scholar, more powerful but if comparing so you must be unsuccessful. There is various types of comparison & if the hatred come out of that so any wrong step can be taken by us, that we can't neglect.

If we want to become successful so we must focus on that how can we become more perfect more than as we are instead of comparing.

There were two types of comparison. One is, I want more than this, & second is why I can't do like this? Means in one side ego is raising & in other side inferiority complex has been raising sometimes.

Take this example. Once we all friends was watching IPL match at one of our friends house. That was Kolkata knight Riders match. In that match Andre Russel was played well & won the match. One of us kept the same hair style like Andre Russel by in the excitement on next day. He beaten by his father so much & made bald. Why? Because Andre Russel's hair style is suiting only on him not to our friend. Same hairstyle will looks good to everyone is not true. Hairstyle is for looking good not to looks strange.

Don't make a head ache to yourself by comparing. If "A" get profit in business & buy a good car so immediately "B" starts to compare. He starts to think quickly that how it's happened with "A"? can only "A" make it? "A" buy a four wheeler car I also think for that. Already the business is not running well & car in that, so what? Car has been loose & bike also. Once two friends was talking after the results of 12th. "X1" said, " I am taking the admission for engineering, what about you?" "X2" replied, "You have 60% I have 74% so I will also take the admission for engineering."

But the funniest thing is that 74% marks has got by doing copy & he was not interested in engineering. But my friend who scored 60% taking the admission to engineering & I have also to take the admission for engineering because I have 74% marks. "X1" has decided already to do engineering. So what was the result came? "X1" all clear & "X2" in first year of Arts after canceling the admission.

Once a has gave the gold up to 1kg to his daughter in her wedding day. He also organized well of all the arrangements. But the father of the groom was not happy after all of that. Someone asked to him, because he was the friend of that person so asked casually, " hey uncle why are you looking sad? Your son is getting married not you daughters." That father replied, " oh, did you know that Ramu got a car in his wedding. My son had a good salaried job more than him." Then that gentleman replied, " your son had only a good salaried job but he is not Ravindra Jadeja, otherwise you will demand for Mercedes!" & all starts to laughing.

We are always blaming ourselves by comparison or underestimating others. Even we are also blaming to God.

Once a boy was mate a gentleman in my contact. He was talking while taking a cup of tea, " I & your brother is looking good little bit. Body is also good. Little bit educated. We are doing whatever work which we getting the outside. But after that why does peoples are not giving us their daughters for marriage? Even that "X" is got married after not looking good, not so educated.

That gentleman was laugh first & then replied, " why does you deserve it? girls are not getting just because you are looking good. You are educated, so what about that? You are earning 8-9 thousand. Your family members are fed-up by your behavior, other peoples in village are also fed-up by the behavior of your family. Girls families are observing that how are behaving? How your family members are behaving? You have your own farm but the crop is not coming in it. There were debate is always going on in your home. There is lack of unity in your family. So the father of a girl must be think about that & if he know about it so he will never give you his daughter."

That boy calm down, because he was agreed on that. The again said, " the boy with whom you are comparing with yourself he is not so much educated, but he is authoritative. He managed well his family by doing well in his farm. He had no addiction of tobacco, cigarette, pan-masala, & drinking like you. Don't compare on looking. Stop to comparing & if want to do it so do it on qualities." Then that boy apologies & show his interest to do something. We can't realize the hidden power within us on the time just because of comparison so we no need to compare with any one.

I had one friend. We decided to start a company in partnership. He had one empty place. We was selling the membership cards for saloons. He had worked in that kind of company before. When we was starts to planning then he was good.

But when entered into home he was not working. So I asked, " sir we wrote each & everything. So what is the problem in the typing?" he replied, "oh sir the vision, mission we have that I first try to match with 4-5-6 companies then we decide." That time I was in need so I replied, "okay, but what is the planning of the card? They said, " first I will match our agreement with that card company & credit card company then we make it." 1.5 month was over in that. Slowly the speed of that work was reduced & that company was become just a dream.

I just want tell one thing in this, that we never be want to insistent to check our idea for we want to become like anyone. We are unique & be unique. Our uniqueness is bring us ahead. So work on your uniqueness. Friends don't compare.

19) <u>Keep faith on God, problems shall run away (help will comes surely)</u>

Keep faith on God means not to leave all & keep faith. Surely you can understand this. Why does we need to make this habit that, sometimes we are doing some work & we are doubting that does truly I get the success in this work? We are not being comfortable by thinking again & again. So then you keep doing your work & keep faith on this that God will give me the reward for that whatever I had done. So then you can keep more focus on your work. Then you will be free & starts to do new things. But if you will think for the results again & again you will never start a new work.

This not may be happen, but if fail by mistake so you will lose more. Then thinking, " I was thought this will never happen, I thought this problem will come or will be. Once you get the results then you can't correct that thing again. Life is always keep going on." No retake in the life." So don't try for the perfect scene. Live by enjoying with whatever scene will come. Once you kept faith on God, then no doubt about the results. I heard that there is a miracle if no doubt.

I am not suggesting to follow the superstition. But there is the benefits of this habit. We can get more peace. We can trust on ourselves & others. Now days is no one is trusting on any one. Very strange is this! But the important is to keep trust. If the owner could not trust on his worker so how much he can expand his business?

Just think, you want to give the 100 franchisees, so need to trust on the 100 peoples. If you didn't trust so you would close your business also. The possibility is that.

One great person had opened his university. The Prime Minister was came in the inauguration ceremony. Prime Minister has impressed & said, " Dadaji, you are doing very good work. The peoples of our country is good. If ask for the help so everyone can help." But Dadaji had full faith on God. They replied, "this is the work of God, if he think to keep it so it will be. When God will think to No so it will be close. But will never do this by collecting the contribution." Still that work is going on constantly. How much Dadaji had faith on God & himself!

This is very big example. If want to give a simple example so that is if you start to trust so are getting the miracles in your daily life also.

I want organize the program of Train the Trainer. But I had financial crisis. I was always saying, "I want to learn, I want to become a trainer." But because of the money I can't do that course. The problem of the money was always comes after all of my trying. Then reduce my sadness & to control myself I was saying, " now I will organize the workshop of Train the Trainer. The God will help me & I will them who don't have the money." The miracle of this sentence that 2 international trainer offered me to take 3-4 peoples in the workshop. 'Will provide you the fees if you want or you can learn free if you want to learn.' This was a miracle for me. I gave thanks to God so much. This is the true experience if my life. I experiencing so many miracle of this. If you observed you will find that the whatever good or bad incidents was happened in your life they all was for good to yourself. Because you will be inspired from that. May be you got saved from the lost. But we need to do the work by having faith. Otherwise we are calling that blind faith clearly. The more efforts are need with the faith.

I am telling you the real life story on the faith. I was living in the ISKON TEMPLE, Juhu. That time in the one lecture Prabhuji was speaking, "one gentleman & his wife was worshiping to Krishna. They had lady of their friend. She doesn't worship ever. But she knows that my friend is more worshiping of Krishna. One day they both ladies were talking.

In that that first lady said, " I want to go to the outstation for 8 days. Who will give the bath to my 'Laddu Gopal'? Her friend replied, " keep him at my home. You tell me I will give bath to him." That first lady wrapped the idol of the Shree Krishna in a cloth & give it to her friend. Next day that second lady took out that idol, when she was cleaning it she realized that the foot of that idols one leg is bend while giving it the bath. Now what should I answer to my friend? She was deeply thought. She wrapped that leg of that idol with the bandage & she starts to burn that leg by hot water & was prying that the leg of that idol be heal daily. She doesn't know, she doesn't worship to an idol. But the miracle was happened before that first lady came the leg of that idol were healed. She asked to her friend that how does the leg has been straight of 'Laddu Gopal'? this is already bend. After this the second lady explain the entire story, she was wondered.

This is be amazing, but miracles can be happen for that we need to keep faith.

You can become successful but the faith is need within you. You should keep the faith on yourself & God also as well as.

20)   **<u>Dream big</u>**

I had heard that Mr. Dhirubhai Ambani was saying that dare to dream big. We don't have a dream. If may be so complete poor. So that's why my suggestion is that we have to make the habit of dreaming big.

The dreams of a businessman is must be big. The only person can do the business can dream big. You can ask to any businessman that how is his dream? Everyone will give the same answer & that will 'Big'.

The dreams should be keep motivating to us. They will be inspire us for work. We just have the wishes like, I want the car, I want the bungalow, I want a job.

I had one friend. He is saying, " I am dreaming so much. But even after 10 years that all are still a dream not anyone is fulfilled." I asked him, " what is your dreams looks big?" so his answer on that , " one big farm house, Audi Car, one business & luxurious lifestyle." I replied, " enough is this?" he quickly replied, " why are you asking that this is enough? These are going to complete & you are asking this is enough?"

I said, " so do you have any plan for all of this? Had took any step?" He is saying, " you know that how is my job? All days is going over in that. After coming in the evening friends are calling. Time is spending in that. After dinner I going to sleep & again leave home to next day by 7a.m.

Then I said, " bro that means you didn't understand the difference between the dream & the wish. Hard work is need to complete the dreams. You have only the wishes. Which you want but it doesn't matter to you if you didn't get that. Because this is not important for you which you are saying your dreams. The dreams are not like this. The dreams are not allowing us to be relax. To completing the dreams are not the work of a lazy person. You are dreaming but for that you need to do something. You want to do the business tell me which kind of business decided to start?" he replied, " No my friend." So I said, "friend so forget about that wishes or start to complete that dreams." If your dream is just a wish so think again. Really you want that thing? If you decided to convert that wishes into the dreams, so decide that till when you want to complete it. keep higher goal. Give the time limit, write it down, & try at least. Not from tomorrow but today, right now & immediately.

Once you starts to take action then the difficulties come, if they comes so excitement is going down. But we need to ask a question without getting it down that why does I started it? then your dream will never a wish you will remember & you will start again with the new joy, you will restart with a new hopefully way. Then it will no longer to complete your dream. If you want to become successful, so you need to dream for all of that. So if we want dream so should not it big? Because big dreams is looking impossible in the initially, but are completing. This is proved by so many peoples. Let see their examples.

Let see to the Lord Shree Krishna, he was the founder of religion & he make it. but we are saying he is God, but we need to develop our life by assimilating his qualities. We are taking him like God but neglecting his qualities. This not the insult of our God, isn't it?

The independent empire (Swarajya) was the dream of Chh. Shivaji Maharaj. They was keep working constantly because of that was their dream & got it. they worked hard to complete the dream. So many difficulties had been came & they faced them & overcome. We want to assimilate their qualities to make our life an ideal. We are not taking their dreams. The useless peoples are important for us. Because no hard work is need there, they are also like us.

Amitabh Bacchan sir didn't get work first because of his voice, he was insulted. Everyone know about this. But they kept working hard & result of that now they are become an ideal of all many peoples. Today their voice is so much famous but their success is very huge. But the useless peoples are important for us.

Let's look into the life of Mahendra Singh Dhoni. You may have seen the picture was based on his life. Cricket was a dream. How he worked hard! They worked hard to fulfill their dream. Today the most successful captains are standing in front of us.

Dr. Babasaheb Ambedkar studied under the lamp because of no electricity. Also went to abroad for study. Worked for the peoples. Wrote our constitution. Today, the country is running on the constitution he wrote.

Every revolutionary had dream of get the freedom to our nation. There was a longing in them. For that they try whatever it & bring freedom to the country. Because we are independent today. Today we have to be inspire through their sacrifice & fighting. Till to the end without losing we try to fulfill the dream. But useless people will come between & we will stuck there.

Peoples called mad to the people who dreamed. But it will not be forgotten that only peoples who said them mad were reading their history.

One of my friend was saying that those peoples were very resolute whose dreams were big. He was explaining by the example. There were same peoples cried after the ascension of Saint Tukaram who destroyed his books by immersion in water. So don't take peoples seriously & leave our dreams. But what we are thinking, what he will say? What she will say? & our life is getting over behind this thinking & again we say, "to dreaming is none of our business!" oh! How many times you tried to fulfill your dreams? Thomas Alva Edison had tried thousands of times then electricity was invented. So after trying 3-4-5 times you are saying to the dreaming is none of our business! If this is true so that is not your dream that is only your wish. Instead of losing the hope by saying this say this that, "let's try again & see," try to find what was the mistake & try again.

It will be acceptable for one time that you are giving the reasons after trying, but without trying if you are giving the reasons that is all waste. Actually successful peoples are not giving the reasons. The decision is yours. To become successful dreaming is most important.